5 EASY WALTZES

by Carolyn Miller

Dear Student,

Waltzes are very special dances. They are fun to play. I hope that playing the pieces in this book will help you to feel the rhythm of the waltz and increase your understanding of how to play musically. Have fun!

ISBN 978-1-5400-2594-4

Exclusively Distributed By

WILLIS MUSIC

HAL•LEONARD®
7777 W. Bluemound Rd. P.O. Box 13819
Milwaukee, Wisconsin 53213

Visit Hal Leonard Online at
www.halleonard.com

PERFORMANCE NOTES BY THE COMPOSER

Waltzing Around

When you play this solo, imagine Cinderella and the Prince dancing together at the ball. Play the melody smoothly. The accompaniment (two-note chords) should be played softly. Sway to the music. Dance and be happy!

Faraway Places

There are many accidentals in "Faraway Places." Finding and playing them first will make the piece much easier to play. Then, sing the words, feel the rhythm, and add the duet part!

Dance with Me

This solo is in A-B-A form. The melody switches from hand to hand. This teaches you to balance the melody and accompaniment. (P.S. Don't forget to sing along!)

Dance of the Penguins

The lovable penguins (from *5 Easy Duets*) return to waltz! Notice the key signature. Can you find all the F-sharps? How many did you find? Also notice the L.H. position change in measure 17. Measures 29 and 30 may require a little extra practice. Continue to always balance melody and accompaniment.

The Twirling Butterfly

Notice the phrasing in this solo. The staccato notes should be crisp, but delicate. Observe the A-B-A form. In the B section, the L.H. has descending intervals of 5ths and the R.H. has special phrasing. As you perform, visualize a beautiful dancing butterfly.

CONTENTS

Waltzing Around

Carolyn Miller

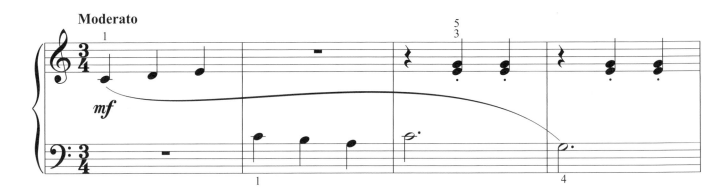

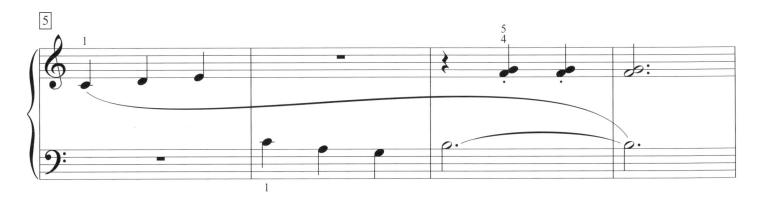

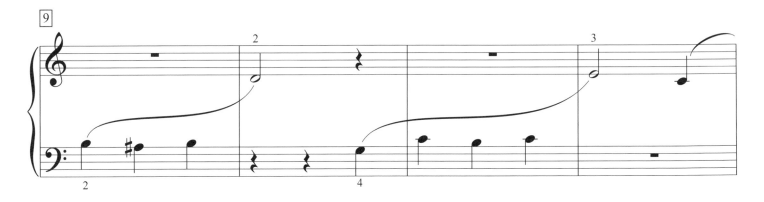

Optional Accompaniment (Student plays one octave higher than written.)

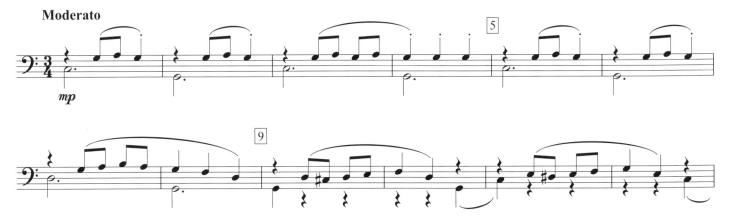

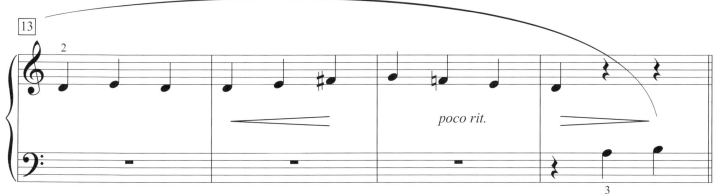

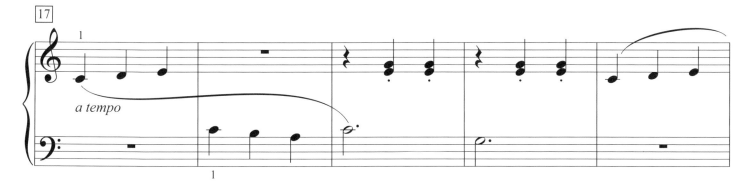

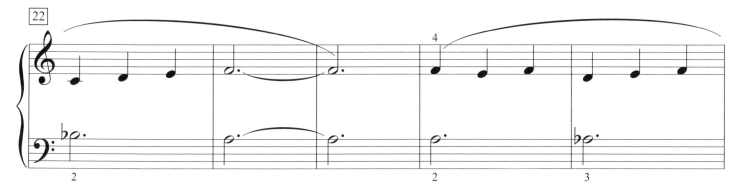

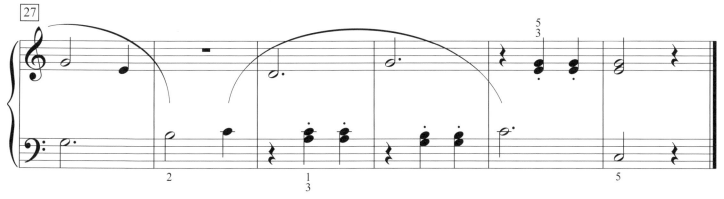

Faraway Places

Carolyn Miller

Far - a - way, far - a - way plac - es.

Plac - es that I want to see.

Tour all the world, sail all the seas!

Optional Accompaniment (Student plays one octave higher than written.)

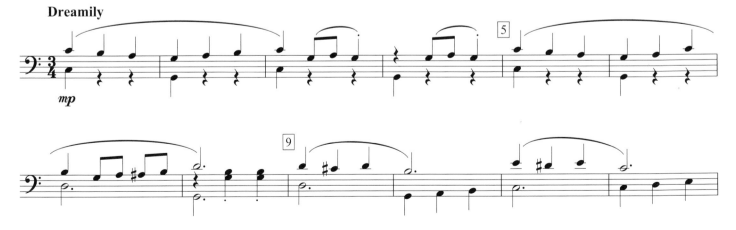

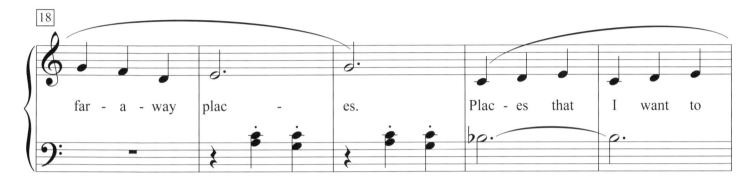

See all the an - i - mals, birds and the bees at the far - a - way

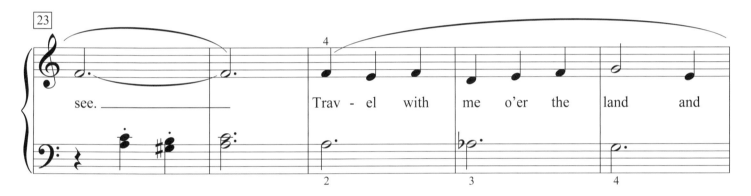

far - a - way plac - es. Plac - es that I want to

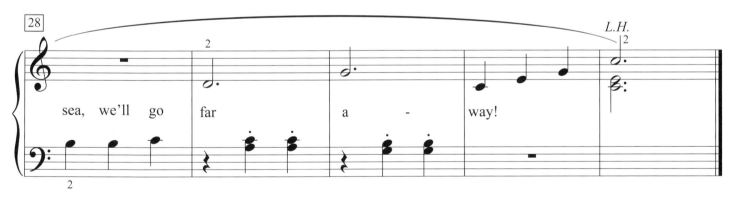

see. _____ Trav - el with me o'er the land and

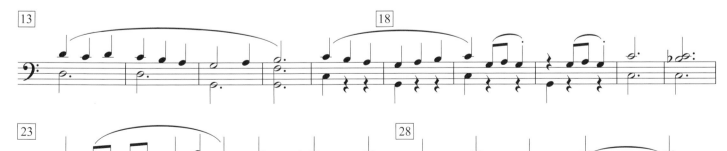

sea, we'll go far a - way!

Dance with Me

Carolyn Miller

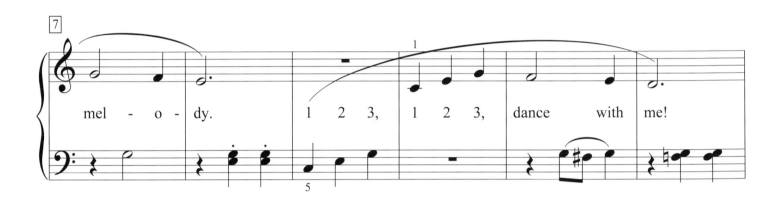

11

Dance with me. Dance with

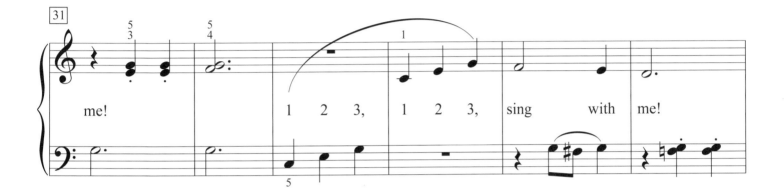

me! 1 2 3, 1 2 3, sing with me!

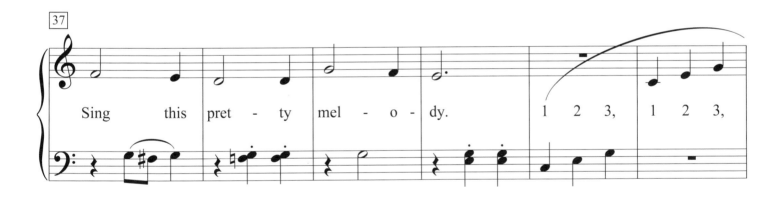

Sing this pret - ty mel - o - dy. 1 2 3, 1 2 3,

dance with me! We'll waltz hap - pi - ly.

Dance of the Penguins

Carolyn Miller

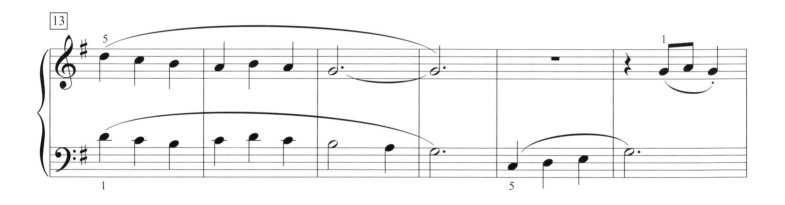

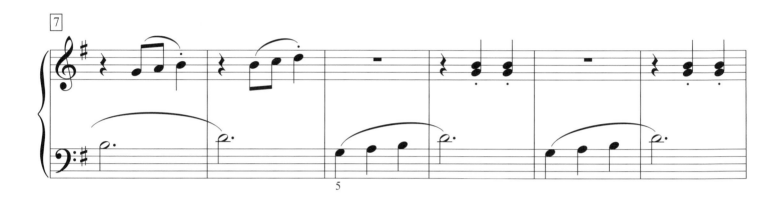

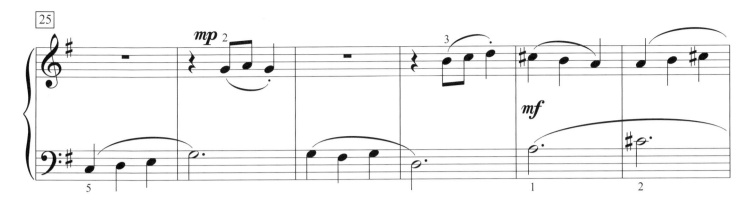

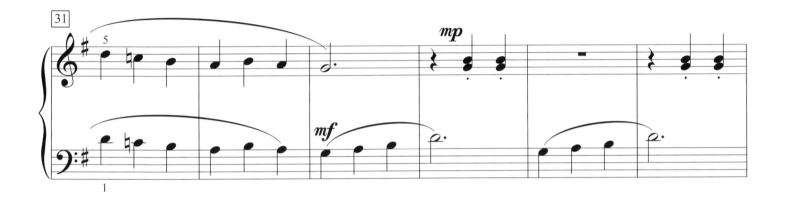

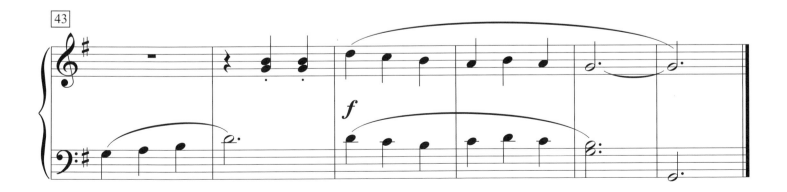

The Twirling Butterfly

Carolyn Miller

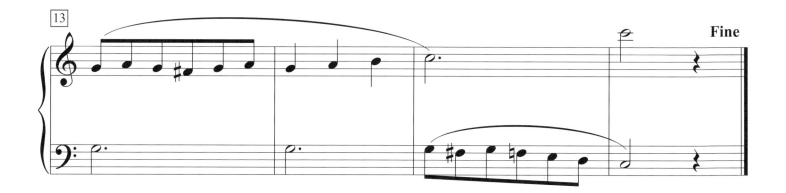

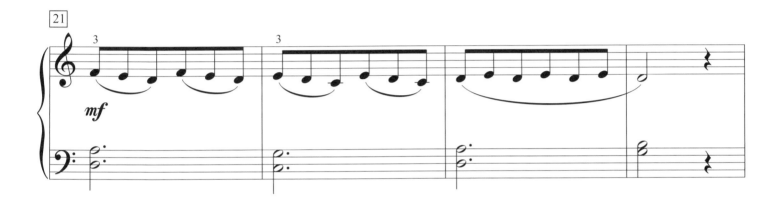

D.C. al Fine

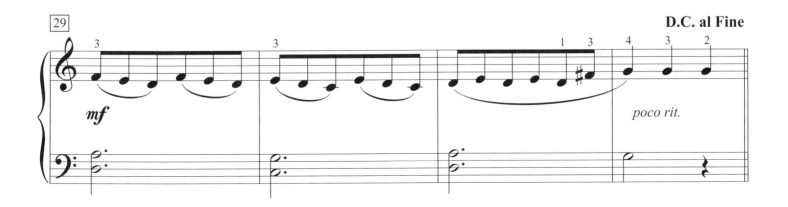

COMPOSER'S CHOICE

FROM WILLIS MUSIC

The Composer's Choice series showcases piano works by an exclusive group of composers, all of whom are also teachers and performers. Each collection contains classic piano pieces that were carefully chosen by the composer, as well as brand-new compositions written especially for the series. The composers also each contributed helpful and valuable performance notes for each collection. Get to know a new Willis composer today!

ELEMENTARY

COMPOSER'S CHOICE – GLENDA AUSTIN
8 Original Piano Solos
MID TO LATER ELEMENTARY LEVEL
Betcha-Can Boogie • Jivin' Around • The Plucky Penguin • Rolling Clouds • Shadow Tag • Southpaw Swing • Sunset Over the Sea • Tarantella (Spider at Midnight).
00130168 .... $6.99

COMPOSER'S CHOICE – CAROLYN MILLER
8 Original Piano Solos
MID TO LATER ELEMENTARY LEVEL
The Goldfish Pool • March of the Gnomes • More Fireflies • Morning Dew • Ping Pong • The Piper's Dance • Razz-a-ma-tazz • Rolling River.
00118951 .... $6.99

COMPOSER'S CHOICE – CAROLYN C. SETLIFF
8 Original Piano Solos
EARLY TO LATER ELEMENTARY LEVEL
Dark and Stormy Night • Dreamland • Fantastic Fingers • Peanut Brittle • Six Silly Geese • Snickerdoodle • Roses in Twilight • Seahorse Serenade.
00119289 .... $6.99

INTERMEDIATE

COMPOSER'S CHOICE – GLENDA AUSTIN
8 Original Piano Solos
EARLY TO MID-INTERMEDIATE LEVEL
Blue Mood Waltz • Chromatic Conversation • Etude in E Major • Midnight Caravan • Reverie • South Sea Lullaby • Tangorific • Valse Belle.
00115242 .... $8.99

COMPOSER'S CHOICE – ERIC BAUMGARTNER
8 Original Piano Solos
EARLY TO MID-INTERMEDIATE LEVEL
Aretta's Rhumba • Beale Street Boogie • The Cuckoo • Goblin Dance • Jackrabbit Ramble • Journey's End • New Orleans Nocturne • Scherzando.
00114465 .... $8.99

COMPOSER'S CHOICE – RANDALL HARTSELL
8 Original Piano Solos
EARLY TO MID-INTERMEDIATE LEVEL
Above the Clouds • Autumn Reverie • Raiders in the Night • River Dance • Showers at Daybreak • Sunbursts in the Rain • Sunset in Madrid • Tides of Tahiti.
00122211 .... $8.99

COMPOSER'S CHOICE – CAROLYN MILLER
8 Original Piano Solos
EARLY INTERMEDIATE LEVEL
Allison's Song • Little Waltz in E Minor • Reflections • Ripples in the Water • Arpeggio Waltz • Trumpet in the Night • Toccata Semplice • Rhapsody in A Minor.
00123897 .... $8.99

A DOZEN A DAY SONGBOOK SERIES

BROADWAY, MOVIE AND POP HITS

Arranged by Carolyn Miller

The *A Dozen a Day Songbook* series contains wonderful Broadway, movie and pop hits that may be used as companion pieces to the memorable technique exercises in the *A Dozen a Day* series. They are also suitable as supplements for ANY method!

Mini
Early Elementary

A DOZEN A DAY
SONGBOOK

Broadway, Movie and Pop Hits
Any Dream Will Do • Can You Feel the Love Tonight • A Dream Is a Wish Your Heart Makes
Heigh-Ho • I'm Popeye the Sailor Man • It's a Grand Night for Singing • Lean on Me
Love Me Tender • So Long, Farewell • You'll Never Walk Alone

THE WILLIS MUSIC COMPANY

MINI
EARLY ELEMENTARY
Songs in the Mini Book:
Any Dream Will Do • Can You Feel the Love Tonight • A Dream Is a Wish Your Heart Makes • Heigh-Ho • I'm Popeye the Sailor Man • It's a Grand Night for Singing • Lean on Me • Love Me Tender • So Long, Farewell • You'll Never Walk Alone.

00416858 Book Only $7.99
00416861 Book/Audio $12.99

PREPARATORY
MID-ELEMENTARY
Songs in the Preparatory Book:
The Bare Necessities • Do-Re-Mi • Getting to Know You • Heart and Soul • Little April Shower • Part of Your World • The Surrey with the Fringe on Top • Swinging on a Star • The Way You Look Tonight • Yellow Submarine.

00416859 Book Only $7.99
00416862 Book/Audio $12.99

BOOK 1
LATER ELEMENTARY
Songs in Book 1:
Cabaret • Climb Ev'ry Mountain • Give a Little Whistle • If I Were a Rich Man • Let It Be • Rock Around the Clock • Twist and Shout • The Wonderful Thing About Tiggers • Yo Ho (A Pirate's Life for Me) • Zip-A-Dee-Doo-Dah.

00416860 Book Only $7.99
00416863 Book/Audio $12.99

BOOK 2
EARLY INTERMEDIATE
Songs in Book 2:
Hallelujah • I Dreamed A Dream • I Walk the Line • I Want to Hold Your Hand • In the Mood • Moon River • Once Upon A Dream • This Land is Your Land • A Whole New World • You Raise Me Up.

00119241 Book Only $6.99
00119242 Book/Audio $12.99

Prices, content, and availability subject to change without notice.

WILLIS MUSIC

EXCLUSIVELY DISTRIBUTED BY

HAL•LEONARD®

www.willispianomusic.com    **www.facebook.com/willispianomusic**